OWNING
MY *shyt*

BY ANITA HAWKINS

OWNING MY shyt

A note to you

Hey, you made it…what a journey it's been! I reflect on my own journey towards walking in my truth and can't help but think about this ongoing process that's led to the happiest and most free I've felt in a long time. I remember the challenges that I faced, the reasons why I fell in love with writing and when I finally decided that this journal was very necessary for not just me— but you too. In the same way, think about why you're here. Whatever you're facing—whether it be a life changing situation, divorce or breakup, traumatic event, extreme loss, or insecurities and fear—it's my hope that this book gives you a gut check, peels back layers, and permits you to hit the reset button so that you can be replanted and grow.

Always,

Anita H

ABOUT THE AUTHOR

Anita Hawkins transcends beauty, brains and business know-how with fierce determination to succeed in whatever she does. As a multi-titled author, entrepreneur, philanthropist, model and mentor, she is a servant first, giving her life's work to everyday people. Anita is known for her global impact advocacy, contributing more than one million dollars to purpose-led work that supports domestic violence survivors, homelessness and poverty.

WWW.OWNINGMYSHYT.COM

Reflecting

Reflecting

Reflection helps you assess where you have come from and where you are going. By taking a walk down memory lane, you can get in touch with who you used to be and allow this insight to help you improve who you are now. These are daily, weekly or monthly reflection practices that move you closer to making positive changes in your life.

Here are some daily suggestions to help:

1. Start a one-sentence journal

A one-sentence journal is the easiest way to start a consistent journaling habit. If you've tried and failed at journaling in the past, try the one-sentence method. It's a habit that you'll love, especially when you look back on a year's worth of entries.

I.E: Sunday, July 2: I talked to mom today and it really wasn't all that bad.

Tuesday, May 13: Just had a fresh shower and finally feel like I'm coming back to myself.

Letting Go

Things don't just disappear on their own. You have to make the commitment to *let it go*. If there is no conscious choice up-front, you could end up self-sabotaging any effort to move on from this past hurt.

Making the decision to let it go also means accepting **you** have a choice. This is empowering to most people—knowing that it is their choice to either hold onto the pain, or live a future life without it.

Express Your Pain — and Your Responsibility

Stop being/playing the victim and blaming others. Being the victim feels good. It's like being on the winning team with you against the world. But guess what? *Get over yourself*. Yes, you're special. Yes, your feelings matter. But don't confuse "your feelings matter" with "your feelings should override all else, and nothing else matters." Your feelings are just one part of this large thing we call life, which is all interwoven and complex. And messy.

No amount of rumination of analyses has ever fixed a relationship problem. Never. Not in the entirety of the world's history. So why choose to engage in so much thought and devote so much energy to a person who you feel has wronged you?

Focus on the present — the here and now.
Choose to live as the victim or live victorious
FoForgive them — and yourself

Forgiving

Forgiveness is for our own growth and happiness. When we hold onto hurt, pain, resentment and anger, it harms us far more than it harms the offender. Forgiveness frees us to live in the present and allows us to move on without anger, contempt or seeking revenge.

Forgiving

Who and/or what do you need to forgive?

_____

_____

_____

_____

_____

_____

_____

_____

_____

_____

_____

_____

_____

_____

Healing

You must be yourself. This means:

- asking for what you want
- setting boundaries
- having your own beliefs and opinions
- standing up for your values
- eating the food you want to eat
- saying the things you want to say

and in a hundred other ways, being you and not somebody else.

Improve
Self-Awareness

Self-awareness and a little soul searching is **critical** to success in all areas of life. Taking time for self-reflection about your life leads to greater self-awareness, which in turn leads to constructive self-improvement. In addition, having a strong sense of self improves your confidence and esteem.

Faith over Fear

Fear & anxiety are the enemy in anything that we set out to do. We are equipped with the power to pursue every idea and dream set forth. It is imperative to not allow your view to be distorted. Have you taken the leap?

_____

_____

_____

_____

_____

_____

_____

_____

_____

_____

_____

_____

_____

_____

_____

_____

Invest in Yourself

You come with attributes, capacities and proclivities that are molded in certain environments. But at some point, you must say, "*Okay, this is original to me and how I have been formed, but who do I want to be now?*"

You'll reduce your emotional distress by deciding to become the person you desire to be:

- a calmer person
- less critical person
- less egoistic person
- a more productive person
- less self-abusive

and so on.

Living Life Vicariously

If you're living vicariously, stop it! Get out and live life for yourself! At one time or another, we've all had the experience of wanting to live through someone else.

Maybe we feel we know what's best for that person, or perhaps we find satisfaction in wrapping ourselves in someone else's accomplishments.

Though this can happen from time to time, it can take us down a dangerous path when it becomes our only source of experiencing fulfillment in life.

Purpose Over Procrastination

"What is my approach? What have I been putting off that's holding me back from my purpose?"

_____

_____

_____

_____

_____

_____

_____

_____

_____

_____

_____

_____

_____

_____

_____

Maintain Focus

How do I maintain focus

_____

_____

_____

_____

_____

_____

_____

_____

_____

_____

_____

_____

_____

_____

_____

_____

_____

Get Moving!

What am I waiting for?

_____

_____

_____

_____

_____

_____

_____

_____

_____

_____

_____

_____

_____

_____

Faith, Hope & Love

What do these three truly mean to me?

_____

_____

_____

_____

_____

_____

_____

_____

_____

_____

_____

_____

_____

_____

_____

_____

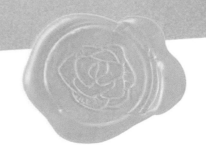

You are Infinite Potential

The important part of this step is that it's obtainable! To create sustainable accountability and change, we need to work towards a process with manageable goals.

You have that power

What are you working on to get better?

_____

_____

_____

_____

_____

_____

_____

_____

_____

_____

_____

_____

_____

_____

_____

Focus on What You Can Change

Where is your energy?

What is your Plan?

Plan A is the plan. Once your foundation is set and your frame has been erected, you are ready to proceed to identify your inner goals and dreams. There will always be doubts and questions but having a solid foundation makes life so much sweeter.

The goals that you implement will change as they are executed, but the foundation set in place to accomplish those goals should **never falter**.

Goals

Setting goals gives you long-term vision and short-term motivation.

It focuses your acquisition of knowledge, and helps you organize your time and resources so that you can make the most of your life.

1. What are your short-term goals?
2. What are your long-term goals?

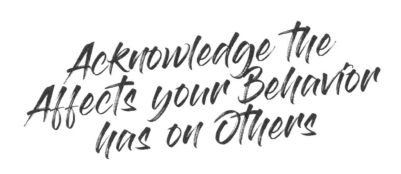

Acknowledge the Affects your Behavior has on Others

Even if we didn't intend to do harm, it's important for us to acknowledge that the behavior was harmful and the affects it had.

This is a step that shows maturity and growth where people tend to naturally make excuses for their behavior. It often looks like: "*I know what I did, it really hurt you, but…*" We have to commit to not making excuses.

Apologize for the offense, own up to it and move on.

Change Attitudes and Behaviors

To make sure that the harmful behavior isn't repeated, you have to commit to changing any toxic attitudes and negative behavior that will hurt someone else. This involves deep self-reflection that may look different for every individual and situation.

Some examples may include letting go of controlling behavior, seeking support to deal with trauma and abuse, dealing with feelings of insecurity or jealous jealousy, and shifting a sense of superiority over others.

Accountability

The first step in taking accountability for harmful behavior is stopping the behavior. Being able to recognize our harmful actions and acknowledge it's impact is crucial; but for the sake of the person being harmed, cease the harmful behavior **immediately**.

After we've done that, we can take time to self-reflect, educate ourselves and unpack the emotions as a result of the experience.

Impact & Exposure

Exposure to the world allows you have impact in the lives around you. You can't be impactful without exposure. How important are your connections?

_____

_____

_____

_____

_____

_____

_____

_____

_____

_____

_____

_____

_____

_____

_____

_____

Affirm Your Real Wealth

What is wealth to you?
Are you rich?

Chance, Choice, Change

What areas do you need to take a **chance**?

What **choices** do you need to make?

What **changes** do you need to make for the better?

_____

_____

_____

_____

_____

_____

_____

_____

_____

_____

_____

_____

_____

_____

_____

Say "I do" and then you'll be able to say "I did"

Who or what is holding me back?

_____

_____

_____

_____

_____

_____

_____

_____

_____

_____

_____

_____

_____

Do What Makes You Happy

What makes you smile?

_____

_____

_____

_____

_____

_____

_____

_____

_____

_____

_____

_____

_____

_____

_____

_____

Learn to Accept Compliments

Do you believe that you are good enough

_____
_____
_____
_____
_____
_____
_____
_____
_____
_____
_____
_____
_____
_____
_____
_____

Renew Your Mind

How can you celebrate
small victories?

_____

_____

_____

_____

_____

_____

_____

_____

_____

_____

_____

_____

_____

_____

_____

_____

If it's Not a
"Hell Yes"
Say "No"!

The body has the innate capacity to heal.

In order to heal, I I had to make a sincere effort to reveal. Thinking positive thoughts can lead to a heart at peace. What are you feeding your mind, body, & spirit?

_____

_____

_____

_____

_____

_____

_____

_____

_____

_____

_____

_____

_____

_____

_____

_____

You have that power

Have you tapped into your capacity?

_____
_____
_____
_____
_____
_____
_____
_____
_____
_____
_____
_____
_____
_____
_____

Reflections from the author

Wow! You made it to the ending wrap-up.

With all that you've written and reflected on, it's my hope that you've found a sense of peace, healing and contentment on each page. Know that nothing happens if *nothing happens*.

Today I am thankful to be SEEN and not VIEWED. It is time—while you have the time—to make that 180 degree complete change in your life. Prepare to reset and make the necessary corrections. Evaluate your current position, who you are, what you're doing and where you want to be. What I stress to others most is waking up with an attitude of gratitude and thankful to see another day. If you are living your life at 360: *spinning in circles, reliving the past, doing the same things, not appreciating life, not being a friend, and living life from day to day; not thinking about the consequences of your thoughts, actions and ultimately how you respond to day to day*—it's time to make a change. If you're not thinking about your thoughts, actions and ultimately how you respond to events—it's time to make a change.

Allow yourself to get a 360 degree view of your life's steps, experiences, and total journey *(the good, bad & ugly)* in order to create a strategic plan to make your change. You may need to let some thoughts, things or people go in order for that change to take place in your life. You have seen the past, are walking in the present, and based on your actions and behavior, you can most likely predict your future. Make your presence count and felt while you can be seen—until the day you leave this earth and **you are being viewed**.

Anita H

Balboa Press books may be ordered through booksellers or by contacting:

Balboa Press
A Division of Hay House
1663 Liberty Drive
Bloomington, IN 47403
www.balboapress.com
844-682-1282

ISBN: 978-1-9822-6231-0 (sc)
ISBN: 978-1-9822-6232-7 (e)

Library of Congress Control Number: 2021901220

Print information available on the last page.

Balboa Press rev. date: 01/23/2021

BALBOA.PRESS
A DIVISION OF HAY HOUSE

Printed in the United States
By Bookmasters